Fundamental Skills to Dominate Binary Options

Jordon Skyes

Copyright Page

CONTENTS

	Introduction	v
1	Chapter 1 Fundamental Analysis	1
2	Chapter 2 How Binary Options Traders Can Benefit From Using Fundamental Analysis	11
3	Chapter 3 Technical Analysis	15
4	Chapter 4 How Technical Works	16
5	Chapter 5 Best Pattern in Technical Analysis	17
6	Chapter 6 Technical Analysis of Binary Options	29
7	Conclusion	39

INTRODUCTION

Binary option trading is a professional activity that requires you to be able to correctly and accurately forecast price movements or at east formulate market scenarios based on fundamental and technical indicators related to the underlying asset. Binary options trading is thus not comparable to gambling. Fundamental and technical indicators will enable you to identify trends and opportunities to accurately time your entry and exit points on a specific asset

When it comes to analysing the market and asset prices movements, there exist two main tools: fundamental analysis and technical analysis. Technical analysis is best defined as the use of charts and historical prices in order to study market price activity and evolution. The ultimate objective is to use this information in order to attempt to forecast future price trends. Fundamental analysis is best defined as the study of macro and microeconomic data in order to attempt to forecast their impact on future asset price movements. It is extremely useful to gain at least a basic understanding of both these tools if you want to get the most from your trading and increase your chances of making money.

CHAPTER 1 FUNDAMENTAL ANALYSIS

The analysis of macroeconomic indicators

Fundamental analysis is the study of fundamental and economic data. There exist a large range of data and indicators that may vary according to the asset class you are trying to study. Major indicators include interest rates, employment figures, GDP growth and inflation figures. For the forex market, more specific data include the variation of Central Banks' forex reserves, monetary policy stimulus, consumer price indices evolution... For the equity stocks and index market, more specific data include earnings, dividend policy, merger announcements and Purchasing Manager Indices (PMIs). Eventually, for the commodity market (oil binary options for instance), more specific data will include weather conditions, producers' reserves, and importing countries' expected consumption.

Fundamental analyses work in a different fashion than technical analyses. Those who use fundamental analyses do not believe that assets are correctly priced by their surrounding market, but rather that market and economic conditions such as supply and demand have a more direct effect on an asset's price. The things that affect this supply and demand are the major, underlying realities of any financial market. These are the fundamental factors which affect price such as company earnings for stocks, interest rates for currencies and geopolitical issues for commodities. Fundamental analysis attempts to study these factors in order to establish the general trend of a financial market. Traders can then use this information in order to base their trades.

Fundamental analysis is not necessarily only for longer term traders to take positions with the general trend of a market. For binary options traders, fundamental analysis can be used on a very short time frame such as sixty seconds or five-minute options if the timing of the trade is correct. As the fundamental elements of any market include news and data releases, binary options traders hoping to take advantage of the intraday market movements that these announcements generate can do this with some straightforward analysis and timing. Trading the news is a popular binary options strategy and many traders purchase short term binary options in advance of a news release in order to capitalise on the market reaction once the news has been confirmed. Another way to trade this fundamental information is to wait for the news to dictate the short-term direction of the market and purchase binary options using this momentum to help these trades expire in the money.

When binary options traders use fundamental analyses, they are attempting to more accurately predict the true value of an underlying asset. Once this value is determined, the trader can make their investment based on which direction he or she feels that the underlying asset will move.

What to Look for When Performing Fundamental Analyses

Just as it is with most other types of transactions, the information that can be gained by a binary options trader prior to placing a trade could be the key to whether or not the trade will be profitable or unprofitable.
Several of the primary pieces of information that are used when conducting fundamental analyses include sources such as:

Economy - Economic criteria can be critical in conducting fundamental analyses. For example, if a particular country is performing well, its tax revenues will generally be high, its exports will be good, and the country's currency will typically rise in value in comparison to other countries that are less successful. In many instances, these positive economic factors can also have a positive impact on the share prices of the major corporations that are located in that demographic area. Conversely, a country that is performing poorly will oftentimes suffer falling currency values as well as budget deficits. However, in an attempt to counter the pressures of inflation, a poorly performing country may increase its interest rates. This tends to result in the country's currency being more attractive, thus causing the exchange rate to rise.

Markets and Industries – Traders who are considering the underlying assets that are related to their binary options trades should also research the industry in which that particular asset lies. In many ways, a company's performance can be tied to the industry in which it is located, potentially causing its share price to rise or fall. For example, companies that are in struggling industries will typically have falling share prices. However, if a particular industry is in a period of upswing, some struggling companies can perform well in the long run.

Indicators - Binary options traders who are performing fundamental analyses should also pay close attention to published indicators, as these can affect asset prices. Leading indicators will actually begin to change before the overall economy does. These indicators can include stock market returns. Conversely, lagging indicators will typically follow at some time after the changes in the economy take place. One of the most prominent lagging indicators is the rate of employment in an economy. A third type of indicator, coincident indicators, can include a country's Gross Domestic Product, or GDP. These indicators will generally move in line with the overall economy.

Fundamental analysis in binary options trading is of great importance if you invest in options.

Rise and fall of the stock prices depend on supply and demand. Therefore, market fluctuation forecasting based on the actual global events is referred to as "fundamental analysis".

Traders dealing with currency pairs have to consider the economy and political situation in the country currency of which they trade when they do a long-term forecast. The exchange rate of a currency depends even on the smallest events in the country. Investors in securities should follow the news of the companies, stock of which they trade. For instance, such factors as management and staff changes, release of the revenue reports can make an impact on the stock.

Fundamental analysis for binary option trading

From the binary options traders' perspective, fundamental analysis is useful in building up a bigger picture of key themes and trends. Most economic data are scheduled in advance on the economic agenda and economists are freely providing estimates of these incoming data. It is thus not so much the data in itself that matters but the deviation of the released data from the consensus estimates and its evolution compared to the previous periods. This allows binary options traders to schedule their strategy around these events when the volatility is expected to pick up.

Fundamental indicators are the drivers of wider and longer market trends. This is why most binary options traders prefer to base their strategies and entries timing on technical indicators that are more short-term focused.

Fundamental analysis is a form of market analysis in which the analyst or trader seeks to conduct a thorough evaluation of an asset in order to determine that asset's inherent value using economic

and political news surrounding the asset or the country of origin of the asset or market being evaluated.

Assets always have a market value and an inherent value. The market value is a function of the response of traders to the inherent value. If the inherent value of an asset differs from the market value, there is an opportunity for correction when a market moving news item is released. A news item causes a change to the fundamental or inherent value of an asset, which leads to a market response from traders and market participants viewing the asset. Their response now causes the market value of the asset to shift towards the inherent value of the asset.

Using an asset's inherent value to compare with its market value so as to either buy or sell or in the case of binary options, to buy a call or put contract, is the basis of the use of fundamental analysis.

The binary options market is different from other markets because, in addition to determining the market response to a piece of news, the trader must also be able to determine the length of the effect of the news item. Furthermore, the response of the brokers to a news item when order flows are so much in one direction as to make it nearly impossible to match orders is another factor that the trader must contend with. Let us look at how each factor can be handled in the fundamental analysis of the binary options assets.

Fundamental Analysis in Binary Options: Matters Arising

Some issues arise and must be looked at critically by the trader when conducting fundamental analysis in the binary options market.

a)   **What Fundamental Factors Affect the Various Asset Classes?**

Four different asset classes are traded in the binary options market. It naturally follows that the factors that cause a change in the fundamentals of these assets will be different for every asset class.

For commodities, especially agricultural ones, factors such as weather patterns, drought, disease or civil conflict (affecting production and export) will impact prices.

For stocks, traders will be looking at things like earnings reports, mergers, and acquisitions, company news, change of leadership, etc.

For currencies, the high-impact news items on the forex economic calendar will create the shift in asset fundamentals that produce trading opportunities.

Stock indices follow the movement of the listed stocks, so if there is a general sentiment in the markets or there is a wave of systemic shocks, the values of the index will be affected. Of all the assets, the movements of stock indices are the easiest to predict as they usually respond to the effects of the underlying stocks traded on them.

b)   **Length of Effect**

Typically, there is an initial spike, followed by a retracement and then a more sustained response to the news numbers in the direction of the initial spike as traders digest the news better. Those who want to trade binary options assets with fundamental analysis must as much as possible, avoid trading initial spikes and retracements for the reasons we shall give below. They are better off trading the response after the retracement. Not only is this the true response to the market news, but this is the more tradable part of the news response.

c)   Broker Response to News Releases

News releases tend to force the big money traders in one direction. That is why there is an initial spike. While this is a trader's paradise in the highly liquid forex markets, this is a broker's nightmare in the binary options market. During an initial spike, most orders are flowing in one direction, and this cold outstrip the broker's ability to fulfill all trade and payment obligations, as there is typically no counterparty trades to use in the settlements. So as not to crumble under the weight of fulfilling orders and settling payments from profitable trade single-handedly, most binary brokers would simply freeze the asset, making it unavailable for trading.

It is for this reason that traders are advised not to trade the initial spike, but rather to wait for the period of a more sustained response after the retracement. By then, frozen assets would become available for trading once more.

It's important to understand the difference between technical analysis and fundamental analysis. There are always arguments over which school should be used. Today we'll be learning the basics of Fundamental Analysis in Binary Options.

Fundamental Analysis is the study of an asset by taking into consideration all the internal and external factors that have the ability to influence its price. These internal and external factors can be varying levels of data, ranging from company data to global events. Many events are interrelated, affecting the price of different assets and the different asset classes.

It would be near impossible for a trader to know and understand every piece of data that is released. However after choosing a few assets to trade; it is possible with the advent of the internet, to really focus on the assets. Also to focus on the fundamental analysis and events which move them. It is still important to keep up to date with the more general financial and worldwide headlines too so that you place information into a much larger context but areas to look out for when applying fundamental analysis to your trades include:

Fundamental Analysis Type -Natural Events

At a very basic level, assets like Corn, Soya and even Oil can be heavily influenced by natural disasters and weather events. Like with any asset, the laws of supply and demand apply meaning that severe storms wiping out the corn fields in the US will mean a shortage in the supply of corn, pushing its price higher. Some natural disasters are easier to predict than others – a rainy summer season in the UK or Europe will mean that the tourism money received is reduced which in turn hurts consumer spending and unemployment. The flooding in Thailand in 2011 had a major effect on the Japanese Yen, as Japan was unable to export its goods through its favoured export route through Thailand.

Fundamental Analysis Type – Politics

Political events can have a huge impact on the prices of many different assets and that includes war. The tensions in Iran over the last year or so have meant increased volatility for the commodity Oil. Iran controls the Strait of Hormuz which accounts for 33% of all oil transportation and as the world's 4th largest oil and gas producer, when there is a change in the production and supply of oil by Iran because of increased tensions or economic sanctions; this has a direct effect on the price of crude oil.

The effect that politics can have on an asset's price movement extends to governments too. Different governments have different policies which affect key areas like public spending, public borrowing, and growth methods.

Fundamental Analysis Type -Sentiment

The financial markets are often driven by sentiment with a pessimistic market reflected in a downward economic trend. When sentiment amongst consumers is high, they generally spend more boosting other areas of the economy. Fear drives the markets – investors fearing for the future of the Eurozone and the Euro will find other areas to invest in – such as the USD or Gold. It was Spanish debt inspired fear in July 2012 which saw the value of Euro plummet over 1% in one day and pushed the EUR/JPY down its lowest level since the year 2000 and the EUR/USD down to its lowest in 2 years. The reverse of that was when the people of Greece voted in a Euro-friendly government and the Euro rose nearly 2% in one day.

Fundamental Analysis Type - Economic Data

The release of economic data can have an instant effect upon the direction of the markets. Data that is released by governments, companies, and research agencies have different degrees of importance but can have a noticeable effect upon an asset. This is where the use of an economic calendar is hugely important to the binary trader, as a good calendar will not just give the time of the release of important but it will also provide the background to the data release. Key data released to look out for includes:

GDP – Gross Domestic Product – This measurement of the total value of goods and services produced nationally is a key indicator of a country's economic health.

Interest Rates – The interest rate is the amount that the bank pays to people, organizations and businesses that save money in the bank. They are used by the central banks to change the economic situation by influencing inflation, spending, and saving. As a rule, higher interest rates also mean higher currency prices as a rise in a country's interest rate makes it more worthwhile for foreign investors to buy and hold onto that currency.

Retail Sales – This is a measurement of retail sales which can include sales from stores, catalogues and even vending machines but always directly to individual consumers. The numbers come from a sampling of retailers which are then calculated to represent the entire economy. In the U.S. for example, 12,000 companies are used as part of the model. The data is split into a number of categories such as food, clothing, and electronics but excluding cars which is seen as a volatile market and can distort the total trend. Consumer spending makes up about two-thirds of a country's total production so can be very important indeed. It is one of the key leading indicators which should be watched carefully.

Unemployment – If you want to see how good or bad economies are doing then look no further than the unemployment rates. In the US the Non-Farm Payroll is one of the most important economic indicators accounting for 80% of the US total workforce. The NFP tells the change in the number of people employed outside of the government, private households, farms and non-profit organizations. Economies that are doing well have low unemployment but when firms stop hiring and start shedding jobs then this is normally seen as a bad sign for the economy. A good example of this is in Spain where a staggering 48% of all 16-24 years are currently unemployed.

There is a veritable wealth of data being released all over the world all the time creating market movement and profit opportunities. A good economic calendar will keep you informed of all the important events. Events like a central bank leader speaking, or the latest economic sentiment in the Eurozone, but what must be remembered is that fundamental analysis and trading the news is used to best effect when in conjunction with technical analysis. However, for the beginner trader, using an economic calendar to make your trades can be a very profitable strategy.

Prior to investing funds into a binary options transaction, traders typically should perform analyses on the underlying assets that will be involved. There are two primary types of investment analyses that are typically used. These include technical and fundamental.

With technical analyses, investors use the assumption that assets are priced accurately by the overall market. This tends to indicate that any type of change in an asset's value is the direct result of movements and trends that can be predicted by analyzing historical information and charts

Natural disasters, changes in the policy of a country, strikes, and accidents influence long-term market forecast. Monthly regular small changes help investors do short-term forecasts.

EXAMPLES OF EVENTS CAUSING MARKET FLUCTUATIONS

Recently, Toyota suspended production because of an explosion at the Japanese nuclear power station and made heavy losses. Also, the company suffered big losses when a large number of finished cars were washed away by a tsunami wave. The losses caused the company stock to decrease. Meanwhile, binary options traders dealing with AnyOption bought PUT options expecting the price to fall. Investing $1,000, they made $850 free of risk or, in other words, an 85% return.

AND THIS BECAME POSSIBLE JUST THANK THE NEWS.

Apple's valuable senior employees left the company to join its competitors, Google and Facebook. This caused Apple stock to fall and the competitors' stock to rise. These events were covered in the news; all knew about them. As you know, the price can decline or rise for several days, that's why binary options investors could put in the massive capital and made a 1000% return! They succeeded due to fundamental analysis of binary options.

Such events take place in the world regularly; therefore, staying abreast of them, you can always catch a good moment for a profitable trade.

Bad news makes prices fall, good news pushes them up. Fundamental analysis in binary options trading will help you increase your profit.

Trading binary options, you need to have in mind that there are two directions in fundamental analysis, namely:
- Right in time
- Long-term reaction
- Right in time

is an immediate reaction to news which means that immediately after the news release the price either soars or plummets. During this period, you can make a profit on short-term binary options. However, you need to react within 5 to 15 minutes, otherwise, you lose the opportunity.

Long-term reaction

After the first 15 minutes, you buy a long-term binary option for a period of a day to a week. The first bounce is a result of a traders' reaction, and then price moves more or less steadily.

The trading of binary options has become open to investors – both new and experienced – due to its simplicity and ease. Yet, even though traders can typically make investments in binary options from the comfort of their home computers, this type of trading still involves some risk – so it is important to do an accurate amount of research prior to investing any funds. One way to do so is to conduct fundamental analyses. This type of analyses is defined as a method of evaluating assets and measuring their intrinsic value by studying their financial, economic, and other quantitative and qualitative criteria.

Some of the world's most famous – and successful – investors have used fundamental analyses as a strategy, including the "father of value investing" Benjamin Graham, Warren Buffett – one of the richest men in the world, and Peter Lynch one of the best mutual fund managers in history.

How Fundamental Analyses Works

Fundamental analyses work by first determining which factors may have the strongest correlating effect on the performance of the asset in question. It is important to note that these factors are likely to differ, depending upon the specific asset that is being analyzed. For example, certain types of companies will perform better than others during times of high-interest rates. Likewise, a particular company may or may not benefit from changes in a country's monetary exchange rates.

When using fundamental analyses, traders are essentially making an attempt to measure any and all factors that could have an effect on the asset's price. These may include asset-specific information such as the underlying company itself, as well as macroeconomic information such as the asset's industry and the overall economy.

Once a trader knows what to look for, they will be able to perform a more in-depth study. This can also allow the trader to analyze potential investments from different perspectives, using both intuition and logic to come up with a buying decision.

An alternative form of conducting analyses is referred to as technical analyses. This is the study of past prices, along with trading volume information, in order to assist a trader in making predictions about future price potential of an underlying asset.

Those who make use of technical analyses will oftentimes study "candlestick" charts that outline a pattern of up and down movements of the particular asset. When traders recognize certain patterns on the chart, they can better estimate whether the underlying asset is likely to rise or fall in the near future – and make their investment decision accordingly.

The advantages of using Fundamental Analyses

Fundamental analysis is used by many traders for both long and short-term investments. It differs from the technical analysis in that it looks for the underlying market drivers in order to base trades rather than patterns on price charts. This form of analysis can be considered more reliable in the sense that these underlying factors dictate the supply and demand of a stock, currency or commodity. Unlike technical analysis, this does not rely on the collective identification and interpretation of a pattern on a price chart, it simply reflects the reality of the market. For this reason, it is one of the most reliable ways to analyse financial markets and can be very profitable for traders who learn to interpret fundamental information correctly.

Despite their differences, one of the most popular uses of fundamental analysis is alongside technical analysis to help indicate if a trade is likely to be successful. Knowledge of the release of news or data throughout the day is incredibly helpful for traders and will help to avoid unsuccessful trades caused by, for example, a price swing on the release of this news. Having a basic understanding of the news and major data releases of the trading day ahead, as well as the implications of fundamental information received before can assist traders in making sure that they will be trading with the underlying market. For binary options traders, this is particularly important as these need only to expire fractionally higher or lower than the strike price with the underlying trend potentially making all of the difference.

CHAPTER 2 HOW BINARY OPTIONS TRADERS CAN BENEFIT FROM USING FUNDAMENTAL ANALYSIS

Those who conduct their binary options trades using the internet will likely have both fundamental and technical analyses features available for their use via the software or trading platform that they are using. This can be especially beneficial for those who plan to factor this data immediately into their investment decisions. Using fundamental analysis can benefit traders by allowing them to be confident that they have done their due diligence before blindly putting any funds into a particular investment.

It's almost a cliché now, how mmt brokers lull the simplicity of binary options to prospective clients. They toss jargon like "fundamental analysis", "events trading", "economic calendars" and "NFP" at you, making it seem like trading is as simple checking the calendar for an important release, clicking Call if it comes in better than forecast, and clicking Put if it comes in red.

Firstly, following an economic calendar and trading on events should NOT be confused with fundamental analysis (if only fundamental analysis were that easy!). Fundamental analysis is all the rest of the market research you conduct, all the reading you do every day that gives you context and a clearer picture whenever a piece of economic data comes in. Fundamental analysis is just about the biggest project anyone could ever get involved in, it is EVERYTHING. All countries, all economies, all geopolitics, all news.

That said. You can still trade events without having an encyclopaedic knowledge of the world's markets. But again, if you think it's as simple as Calling a good report and Putting a bad report your begging to lose your balance. Think about it, if it were that easy don't you think everybody on the planet earth would be doing it?

What follows is the simplest example of a real life situation that will help you understand that all is not what it seems at first glance, that this is not a get rich *q*uick thing, and that you're actually going to have to put some work in if you're going to get good at trading binary options.

Last Friday as expected some very important employment data came in from North America. Canadian employment change and US Non-Farm Payroll data were both released at the same time, and were both extremely positive, beating all forecasts. 180,000 new jobs were predicted for the US economy, the reported NFP figures came in at 203,000. In Canada the situation was even more impressive; the market was expecting a decline from 13,200 to 12,300; the actual figures showed a massive increase of 21,600 new jobs, almost twice that of the previous report.

The following are two screenshots from price action on USD/CAD, and EUR/CAD respectively, showing exactly what took place as the data came in.

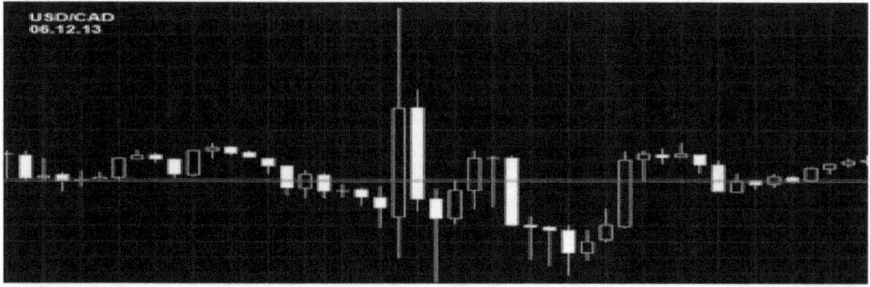

Chart: price action on USD/CAD

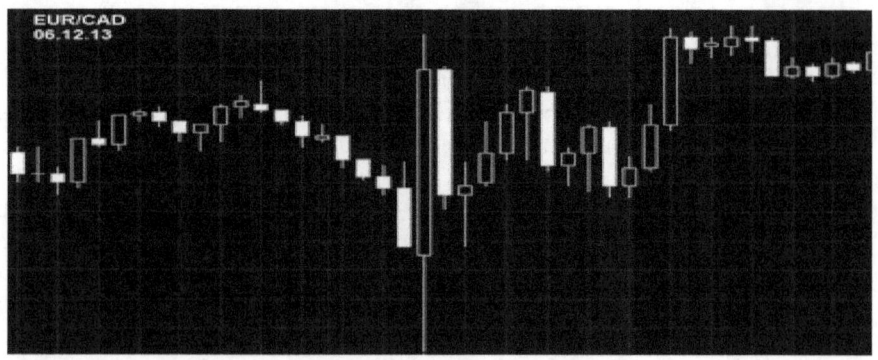

Chart: price action on EUR/CAD

Now, the gains made in employment were much more pronounced in Canada than they were in the US. The US was shown to have only created 3000 new jobs as compared to Canada's creation of 8400 new jobs.

Now look at the charts again, in the first instance USD shoots up, instead of CAD. In the second case EUR, after a momentary plummet, spikes well above the level it was at before the data release (for you binary options newbies out there this means CAD actually went down in both cases).

So what gives? You're always told that if it comes in better than forecast, especially if it's significantly better than forecast, that it's a recipe for some bullish action and some in-the-money CALL trades. Not so on Friday.

If you had gone in with that kind of simplistic logic then you'd have bet big and lost big. Allow me to explain in a few simple points why CAD didn't react the way you may have been expecting it to:

Firstly the US data is always bound to take precedence, and the fact that US data also came in very positive leads me to believe that CAD performed weaker due to the market anticipating an end to QE in the US, and so rallied around this high impact economic report, instead of the Canadian one.

Now that's the simplest interpretation. When you actually look at the data, while employment was up in Canada, the actual amount of hours worked went down by 0.2 percent.

Also, the jobs created in Canada have mostly been in the private sector. The government has been axing public sector jobs like there's no tomorrow (a drop of 1.2%). Also, self-employment accounts for a sizable amount of the new jobs created, which has led investors to further question the quality of Canada's labour market.

Jobs for young people are also falling in Canada, and more employers are opting to hire individuals on a part-time or interim basis. More evidence that the stats look much better than they actually are for the economy.

As you can see, the reality when you look a little closer is quite different than the one you think you see when your research only goes as deep as the stats on your economic calendar.

The things I have just explained to you were factored in by the market, which had the jump on you, and your lack of research, your shoddy grasp of fundamental analysis, would've led you to make an erroneous choice just when you thought you had a sure bet on your hand. THIS is why fundamental analysis, REAL FUNDAMENTAL ANALYSIS, is so important. It provides you with much more resolution and gives you a far clearer insight into the collective mind of all traders on your market.

Do your research, know the underlying trends and the situation on the ground, at least as it relates to a couple of your most traded assets, then and only then go in. That's what makes the difference between a binary trader, and someone who goes in blind.

CHAPTER 3 TECHNICAL ANALYSIS

WHAT IS TECHNICAL ANALYSIS

Thanks to its ease of entry, as well as its lower cost of entry, the binary options market can hold profit potential for both new and experienced traders alike. However, even though binary options trading methods are not as complex as some other forms of investing, the potential for trade benefit can increase greatly through the use of technical analyses.

Technical analyses are defined as being the study of past price and trading volume information in order to help in predicting future price potential of various assets. This type of analyses has been used for many years, and it traces its beginnings back several hundred years to when it was used by rice traders in Japan. By studying the rise and fall of past prices, these early rice traders were oftentimes able to accurately predict future prices – even without factoring in current supply and demand.

It is with the Japanese rice traders that the "candlestick" method of technical analyses came about. This method of analyzing price gives traders a set of symbols that are placed on a price chart, helping viewers to see past price patterns. This, in turn, can subsequently lead traders to come up with predictions regarding potential future prices of the underlying asset.

CHAPTER 4 HOW TECHNICAL WORKS

In many ways, technical analyses involve the use of pattern recognition on a chart. If the price of the asset that is being analyzed appears to be moving upward, traders will see the demand for the company's stock shares that is likely to increase buying – and a subsequent increase in share price.

Technical analysis uses both historical price data, and the study of past price patterns to create visual signals of future price performance. It is one of the most popular and widespread techniques for trading and its popularity also helps it to be one of the most reliable ways to trade. Technical traders spot the early signs that a popular trading pattern is being created by the movement of the price being driven by supply and demand. Once the pattern is complete, the trader knows the anticipated price move in the future and, with the help of many other traders also recognising this, there is a high probability that price will perform as it has done historically with the same pattern. As markets move in cycles, the most reliable trading patterns occur over and over again throughout all financial market. It is by analysing how successful the outcome of each of the historical occurrences is that will make a technical trading pattern reliable.

Conversely, an alternate type of analyzing investments, known as fundamental analyses does not take into account the price movements of an asset, but rather it assesses the overall economic well being of the entity. For example, those who use fundamental analyses for trading individual stocks would study the underlying company's assets and liabilities as well as their earnings and expenses in order to come up with a prediction of whether or not there is enough marked demand to cause the stock shares to rise or fall.

How Binary Options Traders Can Benefit from Using Technical Analyses

Many traders use technical analyses for trading stock shares because once a trader knows the underlying asset's fundamentals such as its supply and demand, these criteria are almost always factored into the share price.

Technical analyses are used in trading a number of different assets, including stocks, futures, commodities, and options. Binary options traders can use technical analyses to help them in predicting the movement of underlying assets. In order to do so, the trader will first need to decide the pace at which they wish to trade. For example, some who trade in the binary options arena opt for 60-second expiry times, whereas others may choose a less hectic pace of weekly expiries.

Those who tend to use technical analyses successfully will typically use a mix of both technical and fundamental analyses for predicting their binary options trades. This can provide a more thorough view of the asset's past price movements and its potential future demand.

For traders who use one of the many online binary options trading websites, it is likely that such technical and fundamental analytical features are built into the trading software or platform that they are using. This can help traders to integrate their analyses and trading decisions with making immediate trades.

One thing to bear in mind when looking to trade technical chart patterns with binary options is the availability of a decent charting package in order to analyse price charts. Binary options platforms often provide basic charting but for this form of analysis, and the ability to apply indicators to your charts, it is often important to have an alternative charting package to look for trading opportunities. These are both abundant and also free with most demo spread betting accounts and online trading websites.

When trading binary options, there are two key types of analyses. These include technical analyses and fundamental analyses. Both types have distinct advantages, and oftentimes it is in using a combination of each that can help a trader to best determine how to hedge their trades.

CHAPTER 5 BEST PATTERN IN TECHNICAL ANALYSIS

Many binary options traders use technical analyses in determining the potential future price movements of the underlying assets. In most cases, technical analyses are better used for binary options with shorter-term expiry durations such as 60 seconds up to several hours – although such charts can also be helpful in plotting the potential price of the underlying asset for longer periods of time as well.

Types of Technical Analyses

When using technical analyses to determine the potential price movement of an underlying asset, binary options traders can typically use time price charts and volume price charts. Price charts may be used to help in tracking the movements of all different types of underlying assets, regardless of whether these are commodities, currency pairs, individual stocks, or market indices.

There are also a number of different types of charts, such as bar charts, line charts, and histograms. However, all of these will typically plot the price of the underlying asset either by volume or by time.

Time Price Charts

A common type of technical analyses involves the use of time price changes. These charts will plot the various price movements of the underlying asset over a certain period of time. The choice of the time price chart that a trader uses will depend on upon several factors, including the type of trader, as well as the duration of the binary options expiry.

As an example, for traders who take on short-term trades, price changes at 60-minute intervals or less can help in predicting the price movements that are likely to occur within the next one-hour period of time.

Traders who deal with longer-term transactions may be better to study price changes that have been plotted on a daily or weekly basis. In these cases, traders may wish to see the open price of the underlying asset at the beginning of the period, along with the high and low prices both during and after the end of the time period.

Volume Price Charts

Traders may also opt to study price movements by the amount of volume that has taken place in the trading of the underlying asset. Volume price charts will plot a particular price level after a certain number of contracts have been made or a certain amount of a commodity has been traded. These charts will oftentimes have fewer entries, and will, therefore, have more of a focus on times when the trading levels are more normal.

When the volume of a particular underlying asset is low, it is possible that sudden changes in price could occur if large trades are undertaken on that asset. In addition, an increase or decrease in the volume of trading can be a signal that the price of the underlying asset is likely to move up or down in the near term.

Likewise, the end of a market move is oftentimes indicated by an increase in volume that will reach a peak and then suddenly drop. Any signs such as changes in an assets volume are important to note as short-term price movements in the underlying asset are likely to occur.

Many of the exchanges that trade commodities and other types of underlying assets will provide information about the volume of trading as well as the number of option contracts that have been traded during a certain period of time. Regardless of the type of chart that is used by a trader, however, it is always more useful if the data is up-to-date and in as close to real-time as possible.

Popular technical trading patterns

Technical trading patterns come in all sorts of shapes and sizes. Some take several months to form whilst others can be seen on a 1-minute price chart. The length of time that these patterns take to form are an indication of how influential they are likely to be and will help to determine the expiry time of the binary options. The most reliable technical price patterns are also the most popular. These include 'double tops' and 'double bottoms' as a favoured reversal pattern used by many traders. This pattern forms when price makes a high or a low, pulls back and tries once again. The failure for the price to move any higher of lower on the second attempt creates the potential setup and when this price reverses beyond the original pullback it confirms that a new trend in the opposite direction is highly probable.

Another popular pattern used by technical traders is the head and shoulders and 'triple top and bottom' reversals. Similar to the double top and bottom signals these both form triple attempts for the price to push higher or lower before eventually giving up and reversing. All of these technical patterns can be backed-up and confirmed by using a technical indicator. These indicators are applied to price charts and can show the strength or weakness of the current price as well as the likely momentum in the future. Combining chart patterns and technical indicators can pinpoint some excellent binary options trading opportunities in advance of the price moving in the indicated direction.

DO CHART TECHNIQUES REALLY WORKS

When trading binary options, oftentimes traders will use different types of analyses in order to help them determine important factors such as the potential future price movements of the underlying asset, as well as the ideal expiry time for a particular trade. In doing so, traders can then make a more accurate assessment of which way the underlying asset will move prior to placing their trade.

The two key types of analyses that are typically used with binary options trading are fundamental and technical. While some traders prefer one type over the other, it is generally best to use a combination of the two types in order to help in making a more accurate price prediction of the underlying asset.

What are Charting Techniques?

When traders use technical analyses, they engage in the studying of market prices by using various charts and graphs that track this information. Those who utilize such technical charts and graphs usually believe that most of the information that is required to make a trading determination is included within the underlying assets value. In these cases, studying the action of the underlying assets price will allow the trader to better determine its future moves.

Traders may use various types of technical analyses when determining the potential price movements of an underlying asset. These analyses will allow a trader to study the historical movements of the asset in order to anticipate where the assets price will likely move in the future. Many traders look at chart patterns within technical analysis and there are a number of these that have gained recognition universally for being highly reliable in indicating the future movement of price. The most popular of these are used by both professional and amateur traders alike and represent a high level of probability that the price will move in a certain direction given the historical propensity for this to occur.

Why do charting patterns work?

Charting patterns work for two reasons:

Firstly they represent a visual reflection of the supply and demand in any given market. This affects price and forces it to move around in a certain way on a price chart and forms a pattern to which traders apply a memorable name. Chart patterns such as 'double tops' and 'double bottoms', for example, are actually a reflection of market weakness and therefore signal a potential reversal or correction in price. The fact that price tries to push lower or higher twice, and eventually fails, results in a reversal.

The second reason why price charting is effective is because it is something of a self-fulfilling prophecy. As the most popular chart patterns are known by almost all traders who largely look to trade these, in the same way, it results in price moving in the desired direction. Although this is looked on sceptically by some, chartists argue that the pattern showing an imbalance in supply and demand has to initially form in order for traders to trade based on this. Therefore, traders are simply reacting correctly to what the charts are telling them to do.

Whatever the reason for charting techniques being so effective, it is obvious that it can be a highly profitable way to trade binary options.

Charting Techniques Used in Binary Options Trading

There are several variations that are used in technical analysis. These can include momentum studies, trend following, and mean reversion analysis.

Momentum Studies – Momentum studies, which is also referred to as Moving Average Convergence or Divergence (MACD), is a measure of the market's momentum. This type of analysis will help a trader in determining whether a particular assets momentum is falling or rising. Momentum studies can measure and compare daily moving averages with longer-term moving averages – and if the changes that occur within short-term averages are greater than those that occur with longer-term movement, then the analysis will show that the momentum of the underlying asset is likely on the increase.

Trend Following – Trend following is the analysis of underlying assets historical prices and its moving averages in order to help in determining if the asset is or is not following a particular trend. In most cases, moving averages are determined by dropping the days that are the farthest away out of the overall calculation. As an example, if a trader is studying an underlying asset's 7-day moving average, then the information from the 8th day will be dropped. It is typically possible to define whether or not an asset is following a trend if and when its shorter-term moving averages move above or below its longer-term averages.

Mean Reversion – Traders who use mean reversion in their technical analysis will base their price movement assumption as if the asset will return to its mean – or its average – after a certain amount of time moving away from it. In many instances, traders will use mean reversion analysis when they are analyzing two similar assets.

By studying the past movements of underlying assets, traders can have success in determining the future price of such assets. And, while there are many traders who prefer to use fundamental analyses – the study of an asset's potential supply and demand based on economic and market conditions – those who consistently make use of technical analyses will oftentimes have great success.

Technical analysis : advantages for binary options

Although there exist many approaches used by traders and asset managers to forecast individual asset prices in financial markets, fundamental analysis, and technical analysis are two disciplines among the most commonly used. Technical analysis is best defined as the use of charts and historical prices in order to study market price activity and evolution. The ultimate objective is to use this information in order to attempt to forecast future price trends.

In order to fully understand and dig into technical analysis, you need to acknowledge 3 main principles that lay the groundwork for this practice:

Market prices move in trends

Market action reflects all known information that is available

The past predictive value of price patterns that reflect the bullish or bearish psychology of the marketplace is assumed to apply in the future.

Simply put, technical analysis consists of a set of graphical and mathematical tools that can be visualized in real time on graphics that traders use to help them improve their investment decisions.

Advantages of technical analysis for binary options trading

The technical analysis presents many advantages for retail traders, it requires a lot fewer data, knowledge and experience than fundamental analysis. You just need a historical graph of an asset price and volume to run the most basic technical analysis. We want to highlight the main advantages of technical analysis:

Technical analysis can be applied to all asset classes (stocks (equity), forex, indices, commodities...)

Applicable to any time horizon (short, medium and long-term) and mostly used for short-term trading decision that is the most relevant for binary option traders

Established framework allows diverse markets to be followed at once, the most advanced trading platform provided by binary options brokers allow you to build advanced technical indicators in one click.

Permits the focus on trending markets, as opposed to markets that are not "moving".

Nevertheless, you should always remember that technical analysis is a subjective science, some say its more an art than a science and that no technical indicator will be right 100% of the time. Technical analysis is here to help you formulate a hypothesis about the market direction but is in no way an absolute truth.

As a reminder, the regulated binary options broker that proposes a complete offer in terms of technical indicators and chart analysis is OptionTime. Don't hesitate to have a look at our detailed review of OptionTime for further details.

Technical Analysis : Introduction to Charts for Binary Option Trading

Technical analysis is the graphical study of charts. A financial chart represents the evolution of an asset price over time. There exist different types of charts that convey more or less information about the evolution of the asset price over a chosen period. Please find below a brief description of different chart types used by professional traders.

Line Chart

example-line-chart-binary-option-tradingIt consists of merely plotting the closing prices of an instrument over a chosen time period.

Implications: While this most basic chart is easy to construct, the open, high and low data is not plotted for consideration.

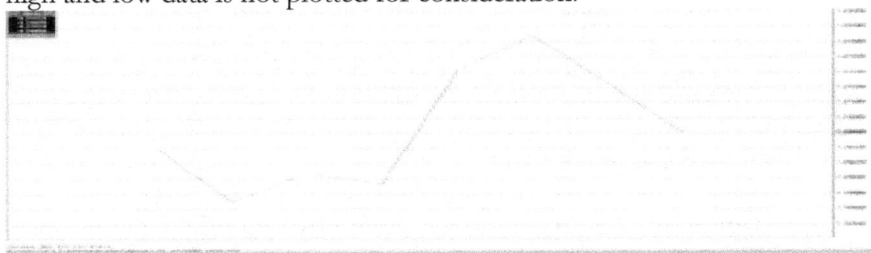

Bar Chart

Example-bar-chart-binary-option-tradingVertically plotting the open, high, low and closing price of an instrument for a chosen time period will produce the bar chart.

Implications: It overcomes the weaknesses of the line chart by including open, high, low and close data for scrutiny

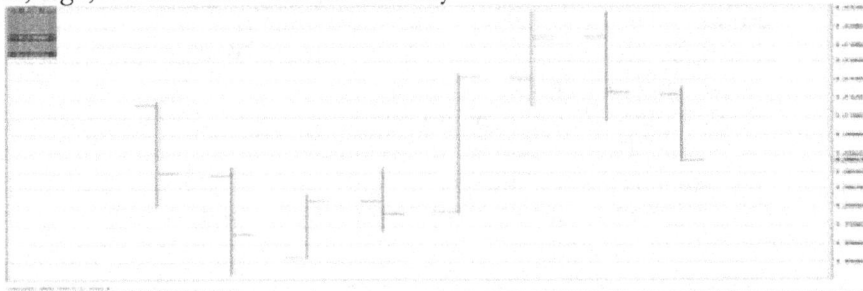

Candlestick Chart

example-candlestick-chart-binary-option-tradingIt consists of plotting the open, high, low and closing values for an instrument. However, the difference between the opening and closing values forms the candle and is termed the "real body". The wicks that protrude above and below the real body are termed "upper shadows" and "lower shadows" respectively. Hollow real bodies are usually used to represent days with a positive net change in price, while solid real bodies usually represent days with a negative net change in price.

Implications: This is the most commonly used graphical representation by technicians as the up and/or down days are more easily discernible.

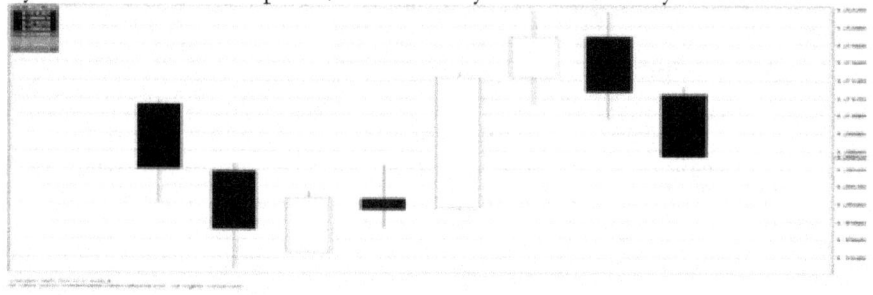

Point and Figure Chart

example-point-figure-chart-binary-option-tradingIt records price changes that are defined by box size criteria. While "X's" and "O's" denote upmoves and down moves respectively, prices must reverse by the amount of the box size in order to be plotted. The example in displays a point and figure chart for USD/CAD using a box size of 10×3. Therefore, each "X" or "O" represents a price move of 10 points, and prices must reverse by a minimum of 30 points (10×3 is termed the reversal amount) in order to be plotted.

Implications: A multidimensional chart format that eliminates the "time dimension" and concentrates on pure price movement. This type of chart is used by the experienced trader and for the analysis of longer-term trends, it is then less relevant for binary options traders and is almost never proposed by binary options brokers.

As a reminder, the regulated binary options broker that proposes a complete offer in terms of technical indicators and chart analysis is OptionTime. Don't hesitate to have a look at our detailed review of OptionTime for further details about this binary options broker.

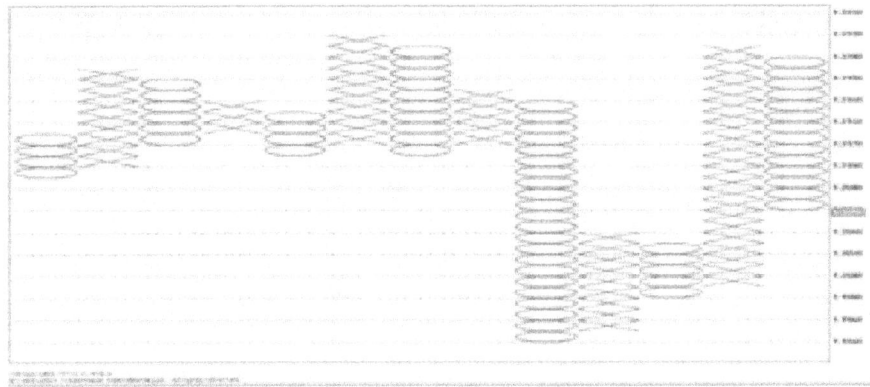

Moving average strategies for binary option trading

Moving averages are one of the most popular technical indicators in the retail trader's community. One of the main reasons for their success is that they are really easy to read and interpret on a technical chart in order to take an investment decision. What is a moving average, a moving average is the arithmetic average of a number of data points over a chosen time period. The most commonly used data points are closing prices. The 20-day moving average will thus be the arithmetic average of the last 20 closing prices for a specific asset. The data is then smoothed daily and is used to identify the beginning or termination of a trend.

How to use moving averages for binary options trading?

The most commonly used moving averages by professional traders are the 20 day, 50 day, 100 days and 200-day moving averages, they use this moving averages on candlestick charts most of the time. The shorter the investment horizon, the more traders will use short-term moving averages to identify potential technical supports and resistances. Moving averages can be used to identify trading trends (long-term bullish trend when moving averages all in an uptrend and vice-versa) but also to determine support and resistance levels on which the asset is likely to bounce or breakout.

Using moving average crossovers to identify BUY/SELL signal

A buy signal is generated in the context of a single moving average crossover when the closing price of an instrument moves above the selected moving average; it is called a bullish crossover. Conversely, a sell signal is generated when the closing price moves below the moving average; it is called a bearish crossover.

Implications: A bullish crossover can be used to implement long positions, while a bearish crossover can be used to reverse positions and to initiate a short position

A buy signal is generated as part of the double crossover method when the shorter moving average closes above the longer moving average. This is often referred to as "the golden cross". Conversely, a sell signal is generated when the shorter moving average closes below the longer moving average. This is often referred to as "the death cross".

Implications: The "golden cross" can be used to implement long positions, while a "death cross" can be used as a take profit and to initiate a short position.

CHAPTER 6 TECHNICAL ANALYSIS OF BINARY OPTIONS

As a trader of binary options, you have to make predictions about future price movements of an asset. In regular trading, there are different ways to do that, but most commonly known is fundamental analysis.

This method examines earnings, dividends, new products, research projects etc. of an asset. Unfortunately, fundamental analysis is not adaptable to binary options. The only way to become a successful binary options trader is to use technical analysis.

How technical analysis can benefit your trading

The more you shorten the time period, the more random and erratic an asset's price moves. These movements are no longer influenced by fundamental reasons but are the result of random, unpredictable events that affect the relationship between supply and demand.

Someone might want to buy a stock because he has some money left over, someone else might sell because he needs money. These events are not always logical and too random to be predictable.

Traders, therefore, came up with a way of dealing with the unique challenges of random price movements: Technical analysis.

Technical analysis is based on three fundamental assumptions about markets and price movements:

1. **Market movements discount everything** -The price already reflects all relevant information that is influencing the price of an asset. It is therefore not necessary to know any fundamental information about an asset. By analyzing the price a trader can find out what investors think about an asset, and where the price will move in the future.

2. **Prices move in trends** -Technical analysts believe that prices move in trends. Trends are zigzag movements in a certain direction, either up, down, or sideways. On different time scales, an asset can go through multiple trends at the same time, often even through trends in different directions.
3. **History will repeat itself** -Thirdly, investors will repeat the behavior of investors before them. That means, although the market movements are random and irrational, they can be predicted if a trader recognizes patterns and draws the right conclusion from them. Two results of this assumption are trend analysis and candlestick patterns.

In other words, technical analysts ignore the question of why prices will move up or down. Instead, they focus on the simple statement that similar price movements have happened before, and most of the time created the same outcome. Therefore, a trader can assume that this outcome will likely happen again this time, and invest in this prediction.

Making good investments, especially on such short time scales as with binary options, is virtually impossible without technical analysis. Any new trader, therefore, has to invest a lot of time to master the basics of technical analysis. Any successful trading strategy for the binary option has to be based on technical analysis.

Trading the binary options, you need to do an analysis of the price movements.

Some inexperienced investors are sure that if the price goes up, soon it falls back. But it's not always like that. That is why the successful traders adhere to the specific rules facilitating profit.

One of the main conditions of the successful investments is an accurate forecast of the price movements. Therefore, before you invest, you need to carry out a thorough analysis. One of the most wide-spread ways is a technical analysis of the binary options trading which we consider below.

The technical analysis of the binary options trading is also referred to as the chart analysis which means that the price charts and the history of their movements are used to predict the future price movements.

The binary options technical analysis is a basic and very important stage of the analysis as it enables to identify the trend type which can be either ascending or descending. To figure out the tendency type and its duration, the financial experts use a great number of tools such as the basic patterns of the technical analysis or indicators.

THE TECHNICAL ANALYSIS IS THE MOST IN DEMAND ON THE FOREIGN EXCHANGE MARKET AS THE CURRENCIES IS THE MOST LIQUID BINARY OPTION UNDERLYING SECURITY.

Trends or tendencies can be divided into three types: bullish (an ascending trend), bearish (a descending trend), and a sideways or flat trend.

In the case of a bullish trend, the price of the underlying rises, so you need to buy CALL options. In the case of a bearish trend, the price of the underlying security drops, hence you need to invest in PUT options. If there is a flat trend in the price chart, you should hold back from investments unless you know further price direction (for instance, you have insider information etc.)

However, the price is rather an unstable indicator, and a tendency can quickly turn to another.

This is shown as waves in the charts.

The other basic term of the technical analysis is volatility which means the price variability or the amount by which the price changes. The stronger the volatility is, the more unstable the price movements are. The lesser volatility of the underlying is, the more stable the price is.

A great number of rules, criteria and laws have been added to the technical analysis for the past years.

The pattern in the technical analysis is a graphic representation of the price movement based a peculiar principle. Hence, if you see what pattern is forming, you can predict further price movement accurately.

The basic patterns of the technical analysis are as follows:

- The Triple Tops
- The Doji
- The Pin Bar
- The Triangle
- The 3 Little Indians
- The Head and Shoulders

To foresee future price direction, the experts have developed special indicators.

An indicator is a graphic model signaling when the price changes its direction.

The indicators are visualized in on-line charts, so you can just click Indicators and select the indicator you need in the drop-down menu.

You can see how it works in the real price chart on this website.

Any indicator is based on the trend and other algorithms enabling you to anticipate the short-time price trend accurately.

The most frequently used indicators in the technical analysis are as follows:
- Moving Averages;
- William's Volumes;
- Alligator;
- Stochastic;
- Moving Average Convergence/Divergence;

- Bollinger Bands

The above-mentioned patterns and indicators have become the basis of a great number of the binary option investment strategies including a tunneling binary options strategy.

Performing the binary options trading technical analysis by means of the price charts, you can sort out what is the current price trend. Also, you can anticipate its duration whether it's a short-, medium- or long-term trend. Using the main parameters of the chart such as the trend direction, its periodicity, and volatility, you can figure out when you should sell or buy binary options.

To make money trading the binary options, use the strategies based on the technical analysis. You can combine several strategies and signals to enhance the reliability of your forecast.

The rules of the market used in the past are still relevant today, and they will be the same in the future. Therefore, if you use the technical analysis, you can predict the future market trends precisely.

Using Technical Analysis to Trade

Trading Binary Options involves making just simple Yes/No investment decisions. However, a truly successful trader will use a variety of analysis tools at their disposal, both technical and fundamental, to help predict the way the markets will move. Whilst fundamental analysis focuses on how macro and microeconomic forces can influence prices, technical analysis is the method of analyzing statistics and data of specific options to assist in ascertaining the future price direction.

There are a number of different methods used in technical analysis, but they can all be categorized into two studies – objective and subjective. The objective studies comprise trend following methods, momentum methods, and means reversion methods. Subjective studies comprise support and resistance and pattern recognition.

Objective Technical Analysis

- Trend Following

One of the most commonly used strategies in technical analysis is studying past prices to ascertain if a trend has formed in the price of an asset. This can be achieved by looking at the past moving averages of an asset. A moving average (sometimes called a rolling average) is an average in which the most recent days are removed from the calculated average. In a 10 day moving average, on the 11th day, the 1st day is removed from the calculated average.

Momentum

The 2nd most commonly used the tool in following trends is the MACD

– moving average convergence divergence. This ascertains market momentum and indicates if the momentum is rising or dropping. It measures the daily movements in the moving average by comparing a shorter moving average change with a longer moving average change. Should the changes of the shorter moving average be larger than the longer moving average change; the MACD will go up signifying increased momentum. When the reverse happens the MACD is dropping.

Mean Reversion

Mean reversion is a theory that the price of an asset will eventually revert back to its average price (the mean) after moving away from it over an unspecified time period. A commonly used technical indicator used to determine mean reversion is Bollinger Bands which makes use of a mathematical formula to calculate a certain standard deviation centered on a particular average.

Bollinger bands can be used for almost any financial asset
Subjective Studies

Pattern Recognition

This is where the trader looks to identify a pattern which can be used to predict a future price movement. A good example is called the head and shoulders pattern; where 2 shoulders and a head are formed in the charts and typically the market will drop after the second shoulder has formed.

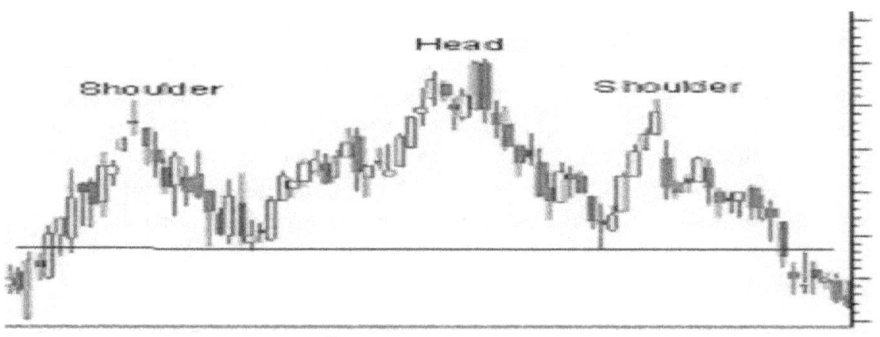

Head and Shoulder pattern in a bullish market, can also work in a bearish market where the graph will be upside down

Support and Resistance

This is a popular tool in technical analysis and is used to determine at which level a price is likely to rise and at what level the price is likely to fall.

A support level is a level where the price is going down and finds support (investors buying). The price then rises from the 'bounce' upwards from this level. However, if the price 'breaks' this level, the price is likely to continue falling until another support level is found.

A resistance level is the other end of the scale. This is where the price goes up until it finds a resistance level (investors selling) and the price starts rising. However, if the price has 'breaks' this level, the price is likely to continue rising until another resistance level is found.

For the Binary Options trader, technical analysis should form an integral part of any trading strategy. Learning the techniques involved in technical analysis can prove essential to a trader when they enter and exit positions as well as keeping track of a positions' risk. Combined with a sound understanding of the fundamentals, technical analysis can be an invaluable tool to assist in trading success.

Profitable 1-2-3 chart patterns to trade binary options

There are a large number of technical chart patterns which appear every day on all time-frames and which can be traded profitably by binary options traders. Several of these can be considered highly reliable and, when they occur, offer an excellent probability of purchased options closing in the money. In order for a trader to effectively identify these patterns, it is well worth having a decent charting package to run alongside the binary options trading platform. Binary options platforms are currently improving the quality of the charts that they offer but quality charting software such as that provided by Metatrader will allow traders to recognise these profitable patterns with ease.

Using momentum and the 1-2-3 setup

We all know that price moves with demand which forms 'trends' which can last from several minutes to several years depending on the chart time-frame. We also know that price can never move continuously in a straight line up or down because of the fact that those taking profits from the price movement and counter-trend traders will always create corrections, consolidation areas and reversals. Binary options traders can use these periods of consolidation as a gauge of the market momentum, to monitor if the trend looks likely to continue and to hop back on when this is confirmed.

The 1-2-3 setup is a classic example of a chart pattern which informs traders that the current trend has taken a breather before moving on higher or lower. The pattern is formed by price moving lower or higher in the direction of the general trend. It then stops, perhaps pulling back two or three bars as if a reversal is about to occur, before surging on past the recent low or high. The pullback often coincides with the 38.2% or 50% Fibonacci ratio of the previous move and the prices failure to move beyond these to form a complete reversal allows binary options to be purchased at the recent low/high as it becomes highly probable that the general trend will continue.

Trading setups using the 1-2-3 chart pattern at a new high or low

When price moves to a new high or low and a pullback occurs it is highly probable that one of two situations will occur. The first is as described above, with a 1-2-3 setup occurring as price surges higher/lower than the recent high/low. The second possibility allows binary options traders to take advantage of a failed 1-2-3 setup through an additional chart pattern.

An example of this is if price makes a new low and pulls back to the 38.2% Fibonacci level before moving towards the recent low. However, instead of moving below this to trigger the 1-2-3 setup, it again moves higher towards the 38.2% Fibonacci level a new high probability trade setup has formed. If a price bar moves beyond the 38.2% level it will form a W shape on the chart and suggest a double bottom reversal has been formed. Purchasing binary options to expire beyond this level is a high probability due to the fact that the downward trend is likely to be over and a reversal is underway.

The Importance of Charts in Trading

Getting started in trading can seem like a daunting task. The odds are certainly stacked against you but that doesn't mean you will not be successful. The only way to set yourself up for success is by coming up with a trading plan. This includes such information as what type of investment you will be trading, what form of analysis, timeframe, risk management, etc. These are important guidelines that you must set up before you start trading. However, this article will be focusing on charts and their potential role in your trading strategy.

Firstly, a trading strategy that primarily uses charts is considered to be a trading plan that focuses on technical analysis. Charts are important because they can tell you where the price has come from and where it could be heading in the near term and long term. However, there are a number of different types of charts, which could have some new traders asking, "Which chart is right for my trading"?

Charts are broken up into timeframes. There is a 1 minute, 5 minutes, 15 minutes, 30, 45, 60, 90, Daily, Weekly and Monthly. For the most part, unless you are day trading, you will be using primarily daily and weekly charts because they are the most popular timeframes and the most widely used. However, as your trading progresses, you can use faster charts to determine the intraday trend, which could lead you to better entry and exit points in your investment. This is key because it can give you an extra little bump in your overall return.

To provide an example, if you are using the daily and weekly charts, always look at the weekly first. The reasoning is because you get the overall longer term trend right and you move to the daily to find an entry point that works well with your trend findings from the weekly. Think of the weekly chart as your strategy chart and the daily as your trading execution chart; where you decide to place trades. Getting into a habit of doing this can help save you from big losses down the road. If the daily is showing bullish signals but the weekly is showing bearish, wait for the daily to turn bearish before you place a trade. That way, there will be less of a chance of the trade going against your position resulting in a loss.

Unfortunately, Binary Options Brokers provide charts just in a very poor quality. The charts are not suitable for advanced trading and chart analysis and you have to find another resource if you take this business seriously. A good and simple solution is a free eToro demo account. eToro is one of the biggest Forex brokers in the world and the broker offers an advanced charting tool including real-time quotes even for demo traders.

A lot of new traders ask me what kind of indicators I use for my charts when I am trading. Honestly, it is simply a personal preference but moving averages, stochastics, and MACD are the basics that you should start off with to get comfortable. Once you feel that you have a good understanding of these indicators and you can easily identify trading signals, move on to other indicators such as the ADX, Commodity Channel Index, etc. It is important that you not jump the gun and overload your charts in the beginning. Remember, a clean chart is easier to identify trading opportunities.

The disadvantages of using charts are over-reliance, not understanding the charts, take the time to learn and not all that easy for beginners. Beginning traders tend to rely too much on the charts, which can get them into trouble. Remember, it takes the time to learn the trade set ups and how to incorporate charts into your trading strategy. It is always recommended that new traders open a "paper" trading account that allows you to place trades but not risk your own money. This will help you painlessly get past the learning curve involved in trading.

The bottom line here is that learning a new strategy takes time. Charts are a very useful tool and a key to success in trading but if you are not properly educated on their use, it could lead to some key popping losses. Educate yourself, open a paper trading account and begin to slowly use charts to trade and see how you do. If after a few months your record is satisfactory, you may be ready for the real world of trading .

CONCLUSION

As you turn into an advanced trader, you'll start adopting a range of advanced trading techniques. One of the techniques you can apply is What is Technical Analysis? technical analysis, which requires the trader to look at historical pricing and/or volume trends to identify patterns that may predict future changes in value.

How to use technical analysis

To conduct technical analysis effectively, you need to look at price and volume data available across a historical period of time. In addition, it is important to combine these price movements with events that are occurring in the market. By matching the market and corporate events with these shifts in value, you'll be able to understand how prices react in the face of market activity. This will help you identify any price triggers that may occur in the future.

Step 2 - Plot Market Activity against Price/Volume Data

After you've gained a good overview of movements in value and volume of the NASDAQ index, it is then important to document any substantial market activity against this information. With the volatile state of the market in recent years, this is an essential step for technical analysis. For the NASDAQ, this could include an improvement in earnings results from the components of the index or general US economic news. It is interesting to review if a pattern evolves in the value of the NASDAQ following announcements of this kind.

Step 3 - Identify Patterns for Future Predictions

Once the data is presented, you can start to identify patterns through the pricing trends in front of you. If you make use of pricing and volume charts, it will be easier to identify these patterns. If a pattern is identified, it is also important to understand if value movements occurred within a predetermined period of time. For instance, if you notice that the NASDAQ seems to increase slightly two days following a US economic announcement, this will give you a strong indication of how the value of the index may fluctuate in the future. Then, you can take that knowledge and apply it to future trades.

Using a technical analysis method doesn't guarantee that you'll see an immediate improvement in your own trading strategy. However, taking the time to look at pricing and volume patterns can help you learn more about your chosen asset and understand how sensitive it is to changes in the market over time. History does tend to repeat itself and learning from the past can often be a good predictor of the future.

www.ingramcontent.com/pod-product-compliance
Lightning Source LLC
Chambersburg PA
CBHW070419190526
45169CB00003B/1321